DANGEROUS MAMMALS

LEOPARDS

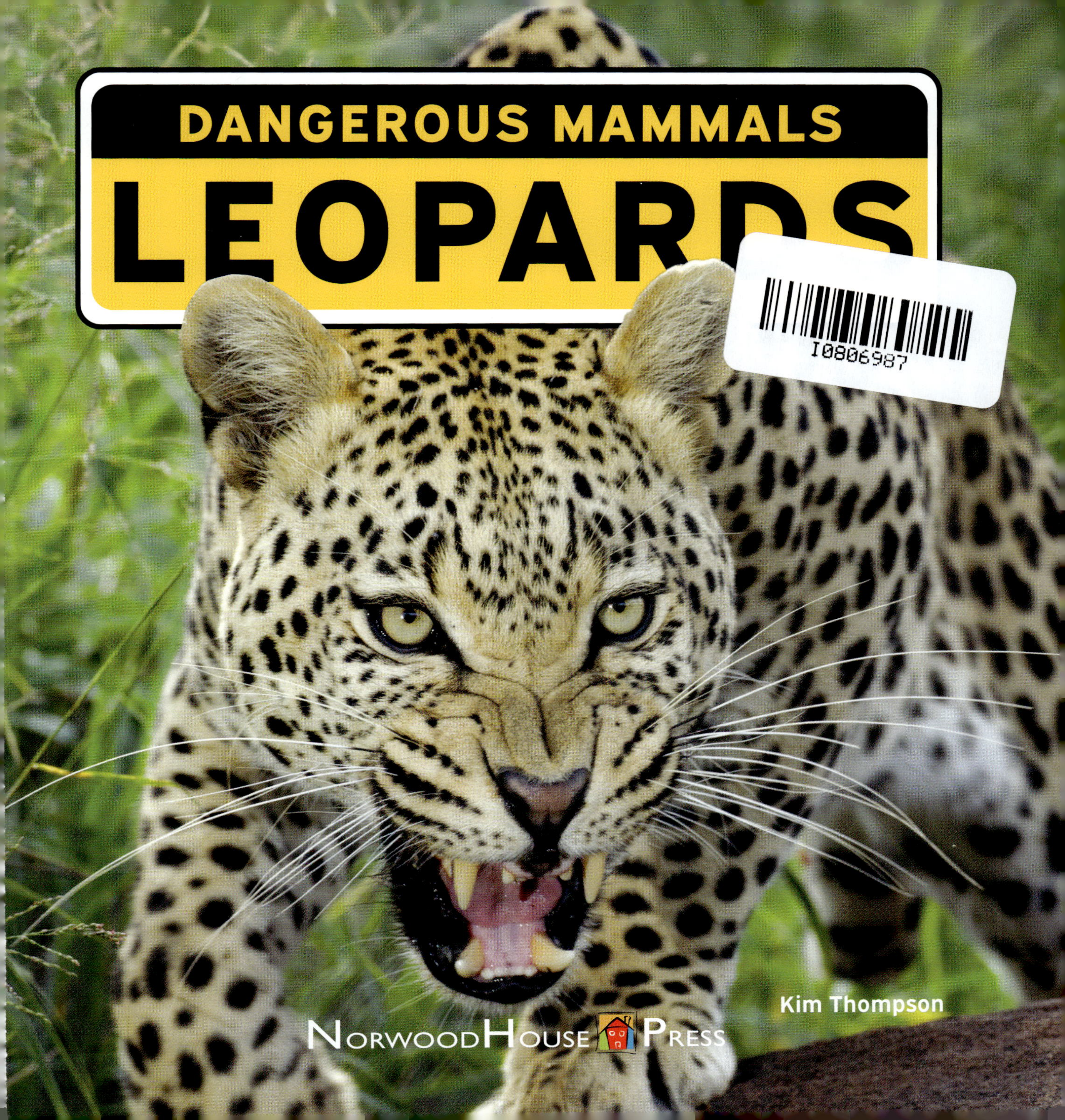

Kim Thompson

NorwoodHouse Press

Cataloging-in-Publication Data

Names: Thompson, Kim, 1970-.
Title: Leopards / Kim Thompson.
Description: Buffalo, NY : Norwood House Press, 2026. | Series: Dangerous mammals | Includes glossary and index.
Identifiers: ISBN 9781978577558 (pbk.) | ISBN 9781978577565 (library bound) | ISBN 9781978577572 (ebook)
Subjects: LCSH: Leopard--Juvenile literature.
Classification: LCC QL737.C23 T474 2026 | DDC 599.7554--dc23

Published in 2026 by
Norwood House Press
2544 Clinton Street
Buffalo, NY 14224

Designer: Rhea Magaro

Photo credits: Cover, p. 1 Stu Porter/Shutterstock.com; p. 6 Holly S Cannon/Shutterstock.com; p. 8 Philippe Clement/Shutterstock.com; p. 9 Sourabh Bharti/Shutterstock.com; p. 10 Vilgot Dietrichson/Shutterstock.com; p. 10 Hyserb/Shutterstock.com; pp. 11, 16 Nick Dale Photo/Shutterstock.com; p. 11 Kashan Hashmi/Shutterstock.com; p. 13 Villiers Steyn/Shutterstock.com; p. 14 GUDKOV ANDREY/Shutterstock.com; p. 15 MintImages/Shutterstock.com; p. 16 slowmotiongli/Shutterstock.com; p. 21 sirtravelalot/Shutterstock.com

Printed in the United States of America

CPSIA compliance information: Batch #CWNHP26: For further information contact Norwood House Press at 1-800-237-9932.

TABLE OF CONTENTS

MEET THE LEOPARD

Leopards are big cats. These **mammals** have light yellow and orange fur.

Their black spots are shaped like roses. Scientists call them rosettes.

Leopards are big and powerful. They can weigh more than 160 pounds (73 kilograms). They can grow 10 feet (three meters) long. They can leap forward 20 feet (six meters).

TYPES OF LEOPARDS

There are nine kinds of leopards. Many are **endangered**.

Sri Lankan and Javan leopards are found only on islands in Asia. North-Chinese, Indochinese, and Indian leopards also live in Asia.

Persian and Arabian leopards live in Middle Eastern countries such as Iran and Saudi Arabia.

Arabian Leopard

Persian Leopard

Amur leopards are found in and around Russia.

African leopards live across much of the continent of Africa.

FAVORITE FOODS

Leopards live in grasslands, forests, mountains, deserts, and rainforests. They are not picky eaters. The **carnivores** hunt for any animals they can find in their environment.

Leopards hunt alone. They catch small animals such as rats and birds. They catch larger animals such as deer and antelope.

Leopards **stalk** their **prey**. When the moment is right, they **pounce** and bite the animal's neck.

After a kill, a leopard may carry the **carcass** high into a tree. There, it is safe from predators. The leopard can return to eat the meat for several days.

STAYING SAFE AROUND LEOPARDS

Leopards rarely attack people. But sick or injured leopards may be dangerous.

Leopards that feel **threatened** will defend themselves. A mother leopard will pounce on someone who is bothering her babies.

Stay far away from leopards. Make sure pets are safe.

If you are threatened by a leopard, shout and clap your hands. Waving your arms will make you look bigger. This will help scare the animal away.

GLOSSARY

carcass (KAR-kuhs): the dead body of an animal

carnivores (KAHR-nuh-vorz): animals that eat meat

endangered (en-DAYN-jurd): at risk of disappearing forever

mammals (MAM-uhlz): animals that are warm-blooded, have hair or fur, and feed milk to their babies

pounce (pouns): to jump forward and grab something suddenly

prey (pray): animals that are hunted and eaten by other animals

stalk (stawk): to follow or track an animal quietly and carefully before attacking

threatened (THRET-uhnd): feeling scared or in danger

THINKING QUESTIONS

1. Describe a leopard's spots.
2. On what continents do leopards live?
3. What do leopards eat?
4. Can leopards climb? How do you know?
5. When can leopards be dangerous?

INDEX

ABOUT THE AUTHOR

Kim Thompson has been an animal lover ever since she was little. She loves to watch animals and photograph them, especially in the wild. She thinks that learning about animals can inspire people to take actions that help animals survive on the planet we share.